The Purpose Driven Life

The principle of definiteness of purpose, the starting point of all individual achievements.

Napoleon Hill

Available now for the first time, read the transcripts of Napoleon Hill's live, rare recordings - inspiring lectures from Napoleon Hill himself.

This is a collection of live lectures that Napoleon Hill conducted in Chicago. It is said that Napoleon Hill has made more millionaires and inspired more successes than any other person in history.

Preface

Napoleon Hill is the acknowledged master of motivational speakers. The principles and philosophy of success that he outlined in his masterwork, *The Laws of Success*, and his international bestseller, *Think and Grow Rich*, have served as the foundation for every motivational speaker since. In these rare recordings, you will hear a complete and thorough exposition of Napoleon Hill's life-altering philosophy of personal achievement.

More than that, you will gain deeper insight into Hill's philosophy as you listen to him interpret and amplify the seventeen universal principles of success. Best of all, these lectures are designed to motivate you and teach you the goals and strategies that will carry you to new heights of personal success, turn setbacks into a springboard to achievement, generate attention for your ideas, influence others and improve personal relationships, define your true joy in life, achieve financial success.

This collection is a working blueprint for a life of

prosperity; an inspiring series of audio lectures that will give you powerful tools to achieve your dreams.

The Purpose Driven Life

*The principle of definiteness of purpose,
the starting point of all individual
achievements.*

Now then, let's break down the lesson on definiteness of purpose and see exactly what it means; why it's the starting point of all achievement - because it *is* the starting point of all individual achievements. And a definite purpose must be accompanied by a definite plan for its attainment, followed by appropriate action. Now you have to have a purpose, you have to have a plan, and you have to start putting that plan into action.

And ladies and gentlemen, it's not too important that your plan be sound. It is in fact not too important, because if you find that you've adopted a plan that's not sound, that's not working, you can always change it; you can modify your plan. But it is very important that you be definite about what it is you're going after, what your purpose is. That must be very definite. There can be no ifs or ands about it, and you'll see before you get through this lesson why it's got to be definite.

Now just to understand this philosophy, to read it or to hear me talk about it, wouldn't be of very much value to you. The value will come when you begin to form your own patterns out of this philosophy and put it into work in your daily lives: in your business, in your professions, in your jobs or in your human relations. That's where the benefits will really come.

The second premise: All individual achievements are the results of a motive or a combination of motives. I just want to impress upon you that you have no right to ask anybody to do anything at any time without...what?

Without giving that person an adequate motive; and incidentally, that's the work of all salesmanship -- the ability to plant in the mind of the prospective buyer an adequate motive for his buying; learning to deal with people by planting in their minds adequate motives while they're doing the things you want them to do.

Now, there are a lot of people who call themselves salesmen who have never heard of the mind basic motives; who do not know that they have no right to ask for a sale until they have planted a motive in the mind of the buyer for his buying.

The third premise: Any dominating idea, plan or purpose held in the mind through repetition of thought -- any dominating idea, plan or purpose held in the mind through repetition of thought, and emotionalized with a burning desire for its realization, is taken over by the subconscious section of the mind and acted upon through whatever natural and logical means that may be available.

Now, in that paragraph you've got a tremendous lesson in psychology. If you want the mind to pick up an idea and to form a habit so that the mind will automatically act upon that idea, you've got to tell the mind what you want over and over and over again; no end to it.

When Mr. Coue came over here some years ago with his famous formula, "Day by day, in every way, I'm getting better and better", he cured thousands of people, but a very great number more than that he didn't cure. And I wonder if you would know why?

There was no desire, there was no feeling put into that statement; you might just as well blow in the wind as to make a statement unless you put some feeling back of it -- unless you believe it.

And incidentally, if you tell yourself anything often enough, you'll get to where you will believe it, even a lie. ('Tis funny, isn't it? But it happens to be true. You know, there are people who tell little white lies, and sometimes they're not so white at that, until they get to where they believe them themselves).

Now the subconscious mind doesn't know the difference

between right and wrong, it doesn't know the difference between positive or negative, it doesn't know the difference between a penny or a million dollars, it doesn't know the difference between success and failure. It will accept any statement that you keep repeating to it by thoughts or by words or by any other means. And incidentally, it's up to you in the beginning to lay out your definite purpose, write it out so that it can be understood, memorize it, and start repeating it day in and day out until your subconscious mind picks it up and automatically acts upon it.

Now, this is going to take a little time. You can't expect to undo overnight what you've been doing to your subconscious mind back bound through the years by allowing negative thoughts to get into it. You can't expect that to happen overnight. But you will find that if you emotionalize any plan that you send over to your subconscious mind and repeat it in a state of enthusiasm, and back it up with a spirit of faith -- if you will do that, the subconscious mind not only acts more quickly, but it acts more definitely and more positively.

And the fourth premise: Any dominating desire, plan, or purpose which is backed by that state of mind known as faith, is taken over by the subconscious section of the mind and acted upon immediately.

That state of mind, ladies and gentlemen, is the only state of mind that will produce an immediate action through the subconscious mind. And when I say faith, I don't have reference to wishing, or hoping, or mildly believing; I don't have reference to any of those things. I have reference to a state of mind wherein whatever it is that you're going to do, you can see it already in the finished act before you even begin it.

Now that's pretty positive, isn't it?

I can truthfully tell you that not ever in my whole life have I undertaken to do anything that I didn't do it -- unless I got careless in my desire to do it and backed away from it, or changed my mind or my mental attitude. I have never failed to do anything that I made up my mind to do and I'll tell you that you can put yourself in a frame of mind where you can do whatever you make up your mind to do, unless you weaken as you go along, as so many people do.

Now let's get back to this fourth premise again: Any dominating desire, desire, plan, or purpose which is backed by that state of mind known as faith, is taken over by the subconscious section of the mind and acted upon immediately.

I don't know for sure, ladies and gentlemen, but I suspect that there's a relatively small number of people in the world at any one time who understand the principle of faith; who really understand it and know how to apply it. And even if you do understand it, if you don't back it up with action and make it a part of your habit life, you might just as well not understand it. Because faith without deeds is dead. Faith without action is dead. Faith without absolute, positive belief is dead.

I don't know how you're going to get any results through believing unless you put some action back of that belief. And incidentally, if you tell your mind often enough that you have faith in anything, the time will come when your subconscious mind will accept that, even if you tell your mind often enough that you have faith in yourself.

Have you ever thought of what a nice thing it would be if you had such complete faith in yourself that you wouldn't hesitate to undertake anything you wanted to do in life? Have you ever thought what a benefit that would be to you? You know how many people there are that sell themselves short all the way through life because they don't have a right amount of confidence, let alone faith? Give a guess as to the percentage.

Well, it's somewhere between 98 and 100. The margin who do is so small that I wouldn't begin to guess just exactly what it is. But judging by the good many thousands of people that I've come into contact with -- and you know without my telling you that my audiences and my classes are always above average -- judging by those people I would say that it's well over 98% of the people who never, in their whole lives, develop a sufficient amount of confidence in themselves to go out and to undertake and to do the things they want to do in life. They accept from life whatever life hands them.

Isn't it a strange thing how nature works? She gives you a set of tools; everything that you need to attain all that you can use or aspire to have in this world. She gives a set of tools adequate for your every need, and she rewards you bountifully for accepting and using those tools. That's all you have to do: just accept them and use them. She penalizes you beyond compare if you don't accept them and use them. Nature hates vacuums and idleness. She wants everything to be in action, and especially does she want the human mind to be in action.

The mind is not different from any other part of the body. If you don't use it, if you don't rely upon it, it atrophies and withers away and finally gets to where anybody can push you around. Anybody. And oftentimes you don't have the willpower to even resist or protest when people push you around.

The fifth premise: The power of thought is the only thing over which any human being has complete, unquestionable means of control; a fact so astounding that it connotes a close relationship between the mind of man and infinite intelligence.

Now, there are only five known things in this whole universe, ladies and gentlemen, just five, and out of those five is shaped everything that's in existence, from the smallest electrons and protons of matter on up to the largest suns that float out there in the heavens, including you and me. Just five things: there's time and there's space; there's energy and there's matter; and those four things would be no good without the fifth thing. There would be nothing -- everything would be chaos. You and I never could have existed without that fifth thing. What do you think it is?

A universal intelligence, and it reflects itself in every blade of grass, everything that grows out of the ground, in all of the electrons and protons of matter. It reflects itself in space and in time. In everything that is, there is intelligence; intelligence operating all the time. And the person who is the most successful is the one who finds ways and means of appropriating most of this intelligence through his brain and putting it into action.

This intelligence permeates the whole universe: space, time, matter, energy, everything else. And every individual has the privilege of appropriating to his own use as much of this intelligence as he chooses. He can only appropriate it by using it. Just understanding it or believing in it is not enough. You've got to put it into specialized use, in some form.

And the responsibility of this course, mainly, is to give you a pattern, a blueprint by which you can take possession of your own mind and put it into operation. All you have to do is to follow the blueprint. Don't just pick out that part of it which you like best and discard the other. Take it all, as is.

The sixth premise: The subconscious section of the mind appears to be the only doorway of individual approach to infinite intelligence. Now, I want you to study that language very carefully.

I said it "appears to be". I don't know if it is and I doubt if you do, and I doubt if anyone knows definitely. A lot of people have a lot of different ideas about it. But from the best intelligence that I have been able to use, the best observations that I have been able to make, through thousands of experiments, it is true that the subconscious section of the mind is the only doorway of individual approach to infinite intelligence, and it is capable of influence by the individual through the means described in this and subsequent lessons.

The basis of approach is faith based upon definiteness of purpose. Now there is one sentence that gives you the whole key to that paragraph: Faith, based on definiteness of purpose.

Do you have any idea why it is that you don't have as much confidence in yourself as you should have? Have you ever stopped to think about that? Have you ever stopped to think about why it is that when you see an opportunity coming along, or what you believe to be an opportunity, you begin to question your ability to embrace it and use it? Haven't you had that happen to you many times and doesn't it happen everyday? And if you've had a chance to be closely associated with people who are very successful, you'll know that that is one thing that they're not bothered by. If they want to do something, it never occurs to them they can't do it.

I hope that in your association with Napoleon Hill Associates you've come to know my distinguished business associate Mr. W. Clement Stone, because if I ever saw a man that knows the power of his mind and is willing to rely upon that mind, Mr. Stone is that man. I don't think Mr. Stone has any worries. I don't believe he would tolerate a worry.

I think it would be an insult to his intelligence if he recognized that anything was worrying him.

Why? Because he has confidence in his ability to use his mind and to make that mind create the circumstances that he wants created. And that's the condition and the operation of any successful mind, and that's going to be the condition of your mind when you get through with this philosophy. You're going to be able to project your mind into whatever objective you choose, and there'll be never any question in your mind as to whether you can do what you want to do or not; never a question in the world.

The brain is the receiving set and the broadcasting station for the vibrations of thought, a fact which explains the importance of moving with definiteness of purpose instead of drifting, since the brain may be so thoroughly charged with the nature of one's purpose that it will begin to attract the physical or material equivalence of that purpose. Get it into your consciousness that the first radio broadcasting and receiving set was the one that exists in the brain of man. And not only does it exist in the brain of man, but it exists in the great many animals.

I have a couple of Pomeranian dogs and they know exactly what I'm thinking sometimes before I know it. They're so smart. They can tune in on me; they know when we start off for an automobile ride whether they're going or whether they're not. Don't have to say a word - not a word! Because they're in constant attunement with us.

Your mind is sending out vibrations constantly, and if you're a salesman and you're going to call on a prospective buyer, the sale ought to be made before you ever come into presence of the buyer. Had you ever thought of that? If you're going to do anything requiring the cooperation of other people, condition your mind so that you know the other fellow's going to cooperate.

Why first? Because the plan that you're going to offer him is so fair and honest and so beneficial to him, that he can't refuse it. In other words, you have a right to his cooperation. You'll be surprised to know what a change there will be in people when you convince them with this broadcasting station of yours positive thoughts instead of thoughts of fear.

Now, if you want a good illustration of how this broadcasting station works: You need a thousand dollars real badly and you go down to the bank somewhere, and you've got to have that thousand by the day after tomorrow or they're going to take the car back, or the furniture, or something else. You just have to have that thousand dollars. Why, the banker can tell the moment you walk inside the door that you just have to have it and he doesn't want you to have it. Isn't that funny? No, it's not funny; it's tragic. You carry the matches around in your pockets -- oftentimes it sets your own house on fire.

You broadcast your thoughts and they precede you, and when you get there you find that instead of getting the cooperation you went after, the other person reflects back to you, what? That state of doubt; that state of mind that you sent out ahead of him.

I used to teach salesmanship; I made my living that way for a long time while I was doing the research on this philosophy, and I have taught over thirty thousand salesman, many of them now life members of the coveted million dollar roundtable in the life insurance field. And if there is one thing in this world that has to be sold, it's life insurance. Nobody ever *buys* life insurance; it has to be sold.

And the first thing that I taught those people under my direction was that they must make the sale to themselves before they try to make it to the other fellow. But if they don't do that, they're not going to make a sale. Somebody might buy something from them, but they'll never make a sale until they first make it to themselves.

Every brain is a broadcasting station and a receiving set, and you can attune that brain so it will attract only the positive vibrations released by other people. Now, that's the point I'm coming to and that I wanted you to get. By habit, you can train your own mind to pick up, out of that myriad of vibrations that are floating out there constantly; train your mind to pick up only the things that are related to what you want most in life. And how do you do that?

Why you do that by keeping your mind on what you want most in life: your definite major purpose, by repetition, by thought, by action. Until finally, the brain will not pick up anything not related to that definiteness of purpose.

Now, isn't that a marvelous thought? You can educate your brain so that it will absolutely refuse to pick up any vibrations except those related to what you want. And ladies and gentlemen, when you get your brain under control like that, you will be on the path, really and truly on the beam.

Now let's see what are some of the benefits of definiteness of purpose. First of all, definiteness of purpose automatically develops self-reliance, personal initiative, imagination, enthusiasm, self-discipline, and concentration of effort -- all of these being prerequisites for success of vital importance.

Now, that's quite an array of things that you develop with definiteness of purpose; that is to say, knowing what you want, having a plan for getting it, having your mind occupied mostly with the carrying out of that plan. And if you happen to adopt a plan (and unless you're an unusual person, you're almost sure to adopt some plans that are not going to work so well), when you find out that your plan is not right, immediately discard it and get another one. And keep on until you find one that *will* work.

And in the process of doing this, just remember one thing: that maybe somewhere along the line that infinite intelligence, being gifted with a great deal of wisdom, might have a plan for you better than the one you had yourself. Have an open mind. If you adopt a plan to carry out your major purpose or a minor purpose and it doesn't work well, dismiss that plan and ask for guidance from infinite intelligence.

You may get that guidance. And what can you do to be sure that you will get it? Why, you can *believe* that you'll get it. You can believe that you'll get it, and it's not going to hurt if you say out loud orally that you believe it. I suspect that the Creator can know your thoughts, but I have found that if you express yourself with a lot of enthusiasm it doesn't hurt any…and I'm sure that it doesn't hurt in arousing your subconscious mind.

When I wrote "*Think and Grow Rich*", the original title of it was "*The Thirteen Steps to Riches*", and both the publisher and I knew that that was not a box office title; we had to have a million dollar title. Well, I went ahead and set the book up in type, and the publisher kept prodding me everyday to give him the title that I wanted, and I wrote it five or six hundred titles -- they weren't any of them any good, not any of them.

And then one day, he scared the dickens out of me. He called me up and said, "Well", he said, "tomorrow morning I've got to have that title, and if you don't have one, I have one that's a humdinger." I said, "What is it?" He said, "We're going to call it *Use Your Noodle and Get the Boodle.* I said, "My goodness, you'll ruin me! This is a dignified book, and that's a flippant title; why that will ruin the book and me too!" He said, "Well, whether it will or not, that's the title unless you give me a better one by tomorrow morning."

Now, I want you to follow this incident because it's potent with food for thought, what I'm now telling you. I went in that night and sat down on my bed as I was going to the side of my bed, and I had a talk with my subconscious mind and I said: "Now look here, Old Sub, you and I have gone a long way together and you have done a lot of things for me and some things to me -- thanks to my ignorance. Well, I've got to have a million dollar title, and I've got to have it tonight, you understand that?" I got to talking so loudly that the man in the apartment above me thumped on the floor, and I don't blame him because I guess he thought I was quarrelling with my wife or something.

Well, I really gave the subconscious mind no doubt as to what I wanted. Now, I didn't tell the subconscious mind exactly what kind of a title; I said it's got to be a million dollar title! I went to bed when I had charged my subconscious mind until I reached that psychological moment where I knew it was going to produce what I wanted. And if I hadn't have gotten to that point, I'd have been up there still sitting on the side of that bed talking to my subconscious.

There is a psychological moment, and you can feel it, when the power of faith takes over whatever you are trying to do and says, "All right, now, you can relax; this is it." I went to bed, and about two o'clock in the morning I woke up as if somebody had shaken me real hard, and as I came out of my sleep, *Think and Grow Rich* was in my mind. Oh, boy, I let out an Indian whoop! I jumped to my typewriter and wrote it down, and I grabbed the telephone and called the publisher. He said, "What's the matter...it's 2:30 in the morning". I said, "Yes, you bet it is, with a million dollar title". He said, "Let's hear". I said,

"Think and Grow Rich". He said, "Boy, you've got it!"

Yes, I'll say we've got it! That book has grossed outside of the United States over twenty-three million dollars already, and probably will gross over a hundred million dollars before I pass on. And there's no end to it. A multi-million dollar title!

Well, after the thrashing that I gave my subconscious, I'm not surprised that it really came over and did a good job.

Now, why didn't I use that method in the first place? Isn't that a funny thing -- why, I know the law. Why did I fool around about it and temporize? Why didn't I go to the source and get my subconscious mind all heated up instead of sitting down at my typewriter writing out five or six hundred titles? Why didn't I? Well, I'll tell you why.

For the same reason that you will oftentimes know what to do but won't do it. There's no explaining the indifference of mankind toward himself. Even after you know what the law is, you know what the score is, and you fool around until the last limit before you do anything about it. Just like in prayer: fool around about prayer until a time of need comes, and then you're scared to death and of course you don't get any results from prayer. If you want to have results from prayer, you condition your mind so that your *life* is a prayer, day in and day out, every minute of your life. A constant prayer, because it's based upon belief - belief in your dignity and your right to tune in on infinite intelligence and to have the things that you need in this world.

And so it is with this human mind. You've got to condition the mind as you go along from day to day so that when any emergency arises, you'll be right there with it to deal with it. Also, the definiteness of purpose induces one to budget one's time and to plan day-to-day endeavors which lead to the attainment of one's major purpose.

If you would sit down and put an hour-by-hour account of the actual work that you put in each day for one week, and then an hour-by-hour account of the time that you waste that you could devote to anything you wanted, if you wanted to do badly enough, you're going to get one of the shocks of your life.

We're not efficient. You have about eight hours to sleep, and about eight hours to earn a living, and then you have eight hours of free time that you can do anything you want to with here in this country where we you live. And then definiteness of purpose makes one more alert in recognizing opportunities related to the object of one's major purpose, and it inspires the courage to embrace and act upon those opportunities.

Now, we all see opportunities almost every day of our lives which if we embraced and acted upon them could benefit us. But there's something in us that we call procrastination. We just don't have the will, the alertness, the determination to embrace opportunities when they come along. But if you condition your mind with this philosophy, you'll not only embrace opportunities, but you do something better. What could you do better than embrace an opportunity?

Make the opportunity! That's the idea.

One of Napoleon's generals -- the other Napoleon -- came to him one day and they were fixing to attack the next morning. And this general says, "Sir, the circumstances are not just right for the attack tomorrow." And Napoleon says, "Circumstances not right? Hell, I *make* circumstances! Attack!" And I have never seen a successful man yet in any business that didn't say, when somebody says it can't be done, he says, "Attack!" Attack! Start where you are.

And when you get around to that curve in the road, you'll know can't see by it until you get there, you'll always find that the road goes on around. Attack! Don't procrastinate. Don't stand still. Attack!

And definiteness of purpose inspires confidence in one's integrity and character, and it attracts the favorable attention of other people. Have you ever thought about that? I think the whole world loves to see a person walking with his chest sticking out, walking with an atmosphere that tells the whole doggone world that he knows what he's doing and that he's right on the way doing it! Why you know, people get out of the way on the sidewalk and let you go by if you are determined to get by; and you don't have to whistle at them either, or holler at them or anything of that kind. You just have to send your thoughts ahead with determination that you're going to do that proud, and believe me they stand aside and let you go through.

And the world's like that: the man who knows where he is going and is determined to get there will always find willing helpers to cooperate with him. Now, there's another very important thing. The greatest of all its benefits, that is definiteness of purpose: It opens the way for the full exercise of that state of mind known as faith, by making the mind positive and freeing the mind from the limitations of fear and doubt and discouragement and indecision and procrastination.

The very minute that you decide upon something you'll know that's what you want, you'll know you're going to do it. All of these negatives that have been bothering you, they pick up their baggage and get out. They just move out; they can't live in a positive mind.

Can you imagine a negative frame of mind and a positive frame of mind occupying the same space at the same time? Could you imagine that? No, you can't -- because it can't be done. And did you know that the slightest bit of a negative mental attitude is sufficient to destroy the power of prayer? Did you know that the slightest bit of a negative mental attitude is sufficient to destroy your plan, whatever it is you're doing, carrying out your definiteness of purpose? You have to move with courage, with faith, with determination in connection with carrying out your definiteness of purpose.

And next, definiteness of purpose makes one success-conscious. You know what I mean by *success-conscious*? If I said, it takes one also *health-conscious*, would you know what I meant by that? What do I mean?

Why, your thoughts are predominately about health! And with reference to success-consciousness, your thoughts are predominately about success. The "can do" part of life, and not the "no can do".

Did you know that that 98% of the people who never get anywhere in life and who we talked about a while ago, are "no can do" people? Any circumstance that you place before them or that is placed before them or that overtakes them, immediately they fasten their attention upon the "no can do" part -- the negative part.

Now, I'll never forget as long as I live what happened to me when Mr. Carnegie surprised me and gave me a chance to organize this philosophy. I tried of every way in the world to give him all the reasons I could think of and I had about six, about six reasons why I couldn't do it. I didn't have sufficient education; I didn't have the money; I didn't have the influence; I didn't know what the word philosophy meant.

Well, there were about two others that immediately popped into my mind, and I was trying to get my mouth open to tell Mr. Carnegie that I thanked him for the compliment he paid me, but what was going on in my mind was that I was doubting that Mr. Carnegie was a such good judge of human nature as he had been purported to be when he was picking me to do a job like that. Now that's what went on in my mind.

But there was a silent person standing looking over my shoulder, and he said, "Go ahead and tell him you can do it. Spit it out!" And I said, "Yes, Mr. Carnegie, I'll accept the commission and you can DEPEND upon it sir that I will complete it!" He reached over and grabbed me by the hand and he said, "I not only like what you said, but I like the way you said it. That's what I was waiting for."

He saw that my mind was on fire with the belief that I could do it, even though I hadn't the slightest asset to give me a beginning other than my determination that I would get the assets necessary to create this philosophy. And if I had waivered in the slightest, if I had said to Mr. Carnegie, "Well, yes, Mr. Carnegie, I'll do my best", I'm sure -- I never asked him about this -- but I am sure that he would have taken the opportunity away from me instantly, because it would have indicated that I wasn't too determined to do it.

"Yes, Mr. Carnegie, you can DEPEND upon me sir to complete it!" And you're living witnesses here, although Mr. Carnegie's long since been gone, you're living witnesses that Mr. Carnegie didn't pick wrongly. He knew what he was about; he had found something in the human mind, in my mind, that he'd been searching for for years. I didn't know its value but I found out the value of it later, and I want you to recognize the value of it because you have that same thing in your mind; that same capacity to know what you want and to be determined that you'll get it even though you don't know where to make the first start.

And what does make a great man? Give me a good definition. What makes a great man or a great woman? Do you have any idea of what greatness is?

Greatness is the ability to recognize the power of your own mind, to embrace it and use it! That's what makes greatness. And in my book of rules, every man and every woman can become truly great by the simple process of recognizing his or her own mind, embracing and using it.

Now here are instructions for applying the principle of a definite major purpose, and these instructions are to be carried out to the letter. Don't overlook any part of it. First, write out a clear statement of your major purpose, sign it, commit it to memory, and repeat it at least once a day in the form of a prayer or an affirmation if you choose. You can see the advantage of this because it places your faith in your creator squarely back of you.

Now I've found from experience, ladies and gentlemen, that here is the weakest spot in the student's activities. They read this, they say, "Well that's simple enough, I understand it and what's the use of going to the trouble and writing it out?" You might just as well not have this lesson if you're going to take that attitude to it. You must write it out, you must go through the physical act of translating a thought onto paper, and then you must memorize it, and then you must start talking to your subconscious mind about it and give that subconscious mind a pretty good idea of what it is you want.

And it won't hurt any if you remember the story I told you in the first half of the lesson tonight, about what I did to get my million dollar book title. It won't do a bit of harm if you give your subconscious mind to understand from here on out that you're the boss, and that you're going to do something about it. But you can't expect the subconscious mind or anything else to help you if you don't know what it is you want, if you're not definite about it. Ninety-eight out of every hundred people, taking a cross-section of humanity in general, do not know what they want in life and consequently they never get it. They take whatever life hands them.

Now, in addition to your definite major purpose, you can have minor purposes -- as many as you want -- provided they lead you in the direction of your major purpose; provided they are related to or lead you in the direction of your major purpose. Your whole life should be devoted to carrying out your major purpose in life.

Find out what it is you want, and incidentally, it's all right to be modest (like I am) when you go asking for what you want, but don't be too modest. Reach out and ask for a bounty; ask for the things that you are sure you're entitled to, but in asking be sure that you don't overlook the subsequent instructions I'm going to give you about what it is you're going to give in return for what you expect.

Second, write out a clear, definite outline of the plan or plans by which you intend to achieve the object of your purpose, and state the maximum of time within which you intend to attain it, and describe in detail precisely what you intend to give in return for the realization of the object of your purpose. Make your plan flexible enough to permit changes any time you are inspired to do so, remembering that infinite intelligence may present you with a better plan that yours and oftentimes will if you are definite about what you want.

Have any of you ever had a hunch that you couldn't describe, you couldn't explain away? You know what a hunch is? It's your subconscious mind trying to get an idea over to you, and oftentimes you are too indifferent to even let the subconscious mind talk to you for a few moments. I've heard people say, "Well, I had the darndest, fool idea today"', but that darn fool idea, you know, might have been a million dollar idea if you'd had listened to it and done something about it.

Have great respect for these hunches that come to you because there's something outside of yourself trying to communicate with you, undoubtedly. I have a great respect for these hunches that come to me, and they come to me constantly. I find them always related to something my mind's been dwelling upon, something I want to do, something that I'm engaged in.

Write out a definite clear outline of the plan or plans and state the maximum of time within which you intend to attain it. Now that timing is important, very important. Don't write out as your definite major aim that I intend to become the best salesman in the world, or that I intend to become the best employee in my organization, or that I intend to make a lot of money. That's not definite. Whatever it is that you consider to be your major objective in life, write it out clearly and TIME it:

I intend to attain within ____ *number of years so and so*, and then go ahead and describe *so and so*, what it is. And then in the next paragraph down below:

I intend to give in return for the thing that I request so and so, and then go ahead and describe it.

Now this business of timing: You know, nature has a precision about timing everything. If you go out, you're a farmer, you want to plant some wheat in the field; you go out and you prepare that ground, you sow the wheat at the right season of the year, and then after you sow it you go back the next day with a harvester and start harvesting -- the very next day.

Well, isn't anybody going to catch me up on that one? What do you wait for? For nature to do *her* part!

Infinite intelligence, or God, no matter what you call it, we're talking about the same thing -- but there is an intelligence that does its part if you do your part first! Intelligence is not going to direct you to, nor attract to you the object of your major purpose unless you know what it is, and unless you properly time it. It would be quite ridiculous if you started out with only a mediocre talent and said that you're going to make a million dollars within the next 30 days; it would be quite ridiculous. In other words, make your major purpose within reason of what you know you're able to deserve.

Next, keep your major purpose strictly to yourself except insofar as you will receive further instructions on this subject in the lesson on the mastermind. Now why do I suggest that you keep your major purpose to yourself? Well, the reason of course that you don't disclose your major purpose to other people is that there are a lot of idle, curious people in this world who like stand on the sidelines and stick their toes out when you go by, especially if you've got a high head and look like you're going to accomplish more in life than they are. And for no good reason at all, as you go along, they stick their toes out just to see you fall. They throw monkey wrenches in your machinery; if they don't have monkey wrenches they put sand in your gearbox. But they will slow you down. Why? Because of the envy of mankind.

Now, the only way to speak about your definite major purpose is in action after the fact and not before the fact, after you've achieved it. Let it speak for itself. Let it speak for itself. The only way anybody can afford to boast or brag about himself is not by words but by deeds, and then if the deeds are engaged in you don't need any words; they speak for themselves.

Now about making your plan flexible. Don't become determined that the plan you worked out is perfect just because you worked it out. You will make a mistake if you do that. Leave your plan flexible. Give it a good trial, and if it's not working properly, change it.

Next, recall your major purpose into your consciousness as often as may be practical. Eat with it; sleep with it; and take it with you wherever you go, keeping in mind the fact that your subconscious mind can thus be influenced to work for its attainment while you sleep.

Your conscious mind is a very jealous mind. It stands guard and doesn't want anything to get by except the things that you are afraid of and the things that you are very enthusiastic about -- and especially the things that you are afraid of. It does let those get by sometimes too. But generally speaking, if you want to plant an idea in your subconscious mind, you have to do it with a tremendous amount of faith, tremendous amount of enthusiasm. You've got to rush the conscious mind so that it steps aside and lets you go through to the subconscious because of your enthusiasm and your faith.

And then repetition is a marvelous thing, too. The conscious mind finally gets tired of hearing you say a thing over and over and over, and says, "All right, if you're bound to repeat that, I can't stand here and watch you forever; go on in there and take it into Sub and see what he'll do with it". That's the way it works.

This conscious mind learns all of the things which won't work; did you know that it has a tremendous stock of things that won't work and things that are not right. It has a tremendous stock of old pieces of string, horseshoes and nails like some misers gather up; a whole stock of those things lying around -- useless trash that it has gathered that you don't need. That's the kind of stuff that it's feeding to your subconscious mind.

Every night, just before you go to bed, you should give your subconscious mind some sort of an order for the night; what it is you want done. I should say the healing of your body -- certainly the body needs your praying every day. When you lay the carcass down for sleep, why, turn it over to infinite intelligence and request your subconscious mind to go to work and heal every cell in your body, every organ, and to give you tomorrow morning a perfectly conditioned body in which the mind may function.

Don't go to bed without giving orders to your subconscious mind. Tell it what you want! Get into the habit of telling it what you want. If you keep on long enough, it'll believe you and deliver what you ask for. And that's why you'd better be careful what you ask for because if you keep on asking for it, you're going to get it. I wonder if you wouldn't be surprised if you knew right now what you've been asking for back down through the years. Have you ever thought of that? You've been asking for it, sure you have. Everything that you have that you don't want, you've been asking for it. Maybe by neglect, maybe you didn't tell the subconscious mind what you really wanted, and that stocked up on a lot of stuff you didn't want. It works that way.

Now here are some important factors in connection with your definite major purpose. First of all, it should represent your greatest purpose in life -- the one, single purpose which above all others you desire to achieve, and the fruits of which you are willing to leave behind you as a monument to yourself. Now that's what your definite major purpose should be. I'm not talking about your minor purposes, now, I'm talking about your major, overall purpose, your lifelong purpose.

And believe me, friends, if you don't have an overall, lifelong purpose you are just wasting the better portion of your life. The wear and tear of living is not worth the price you pay for it unless you really are aiming for something; unless you're going somewhere in life, unless you are doing something with this opportunity here on this plane. I imagine you were sent over here to do something. I imagine you were sent over here with a mind capable of attaining your own destiny, and if you don't tame that, if you don't use that mind, I imagine that your life, to a large extent, will have been wasted from the viewpoint of the one who sent you over.

Take possession of your mind. Aim high! Don't believe because in the past you may not have achieved much that you can't achieve in the future. Don't measure your future by your past; if you do, you're sunk.

A new day is coming -- you're going to be born again! You're setting up a new pattern! You're in a new world! You're a new person! I intend that every one of you shall be born again -- mentally, physically, and maybe spiritually. A new aim, a new purpose, a new realization of your own individual power, and a new realization of your own dignity as a unit in mankind.

If you ask me what I believe to be the greatest sin of mankind, I'd bet you'd be surprised at what my answer would be. What would yours be? What do you think the greatest sin of mankind is?

The greatest sin of mankind is neglect to use his greatest asset! That's the greatest sin of mankind! It's bound to be that, because if you use that greatest asset, you'll have everything you want, and you'll have it in abundance. You notice I didn't say you'll have everything within reason, I said you'd have everything you want and have it in abundance. I didn't put any qualifying words in there! You're the only one that can put qualifying words in there as to what you want. You're the only one that can set up limitations for yourself. Nobody else can do it for you, unless you let them.

Your major purpose, or some portion of it, should remain a few jumps ahead of you at all times, as something to which you may look forward with hope and anticipation. Now, if you ever catch up with your major purpose and attain it, then what? What are you going to do then? Get another one, of course! And you will have learned, by having attained your first one, that you *can* attain a major purpose and the chances are that when you select your next one you'll make it a bigger objective than you did your first one.

If your object is to acquire material riches, why don't aim for too high for the first year. You know, work out a 12 months plan within reason and watch how easily you can attain it, and then next year double it. And then next year double that.

One's major purpose should keep a few jumps ahead of him. What's the purpose of that? Why not lay out a definite purpose that you can catch up with, well, just tomorrow say? Well now, obviously if you do that your definite major purpose is not going to be very extensive, is it? And you're not going to have the fun of pursuit! Do you know the fun of pursuit is a great thing! And if you found success, if you found your objective, why then there's no fun in it, but you have to turn around and start after something else.

Life is less interesting when one has no definite purpose to be attained other than that of merely living. The hope of future achievement in connection with a major purpose is among the greatest of man's pleasures. Sorry is the man indeed who's caught up with himself and no longer has anything to do. I've found a lot of them. They're all miserable. No, you've got to keep active. Keep doing something, keep working, keep an objective ahead of you.

One's major purpose may, and it generally does consist of that which can be attained only by a series of day-to-day, and month-to-month, and year-to-year steps, because it is something which should be so designed as to consume an entire lifetime of endeavor. It should harmonize with one's occupation, business, or profession, for each day's work should enable one to come one day nearer to the attainment of his major purpose in life.

I feel sorry, indeed I feel sorry, for the individual who is just working day-in and day-out in order to have something to eat and some clothes to wear and a place to sleep. I feel sorry for that kind of a person, that has no aim beyond just enough to exist on. I can't imagine anybody in this class satisfying himself sitting down on an existence. I think you want to live! I think you want abundance! I think you want everything that's necessary for you to do the thing you want to do in life. Including money.

One's major purpose may, and it generally does consist of that which can be attained only by a series of day-to-day or month-to-month steps. Now remember that when you start in pursuit of your definite major purpose. One's major purpose may consist of many different combinations of lesser aims such as the nature of one's occupation, which should be something of his own choice. When you come to write out your definite major purpose, you write it out like the planks in a platform. Number one is so-and-so; number two, so-and-so. And somewhere along there, right near the head, be sure that you include in your definite major purpose perfect harmony between yourself and your mate.

Think that's important? Do you know of anything more important than that? Do you know of any human relationship more important than that of a man and his wife? No, of course you don't, I'll answer that one for you. Nobody does. And have you ever heard of a relationship between a man and his wife where there was not harmony? Have you ever seen a thing like that? You have, huh? I'll answer that for you too; I know you have. Not pleasant, is it? Not pleasant to even be around people who are not in step with one another.

Well you can be harmonious, and there is where you ought to start applying your mastermind relationship first. Your wife or your husband should be your first mastermind ally. Maybe you'll have to go back and court her or him over again, but all right, that's nice too. I don't know if I ever did anything in my life that I enjoyed as much as courting. It's a wonderful experience! Go back and court the gal over again, or the man. It's a wonderful experience.

Or if you're not on the right kind of terms with your business associate, or your fellow worker, or the people you work with everyday. Go back and rededicate yourself to the business of striking up on a new basis. You'll be surprised at what a little confession on your part will do! A wonderful thing; a confession is really a marvelous thing. Most people claim they have too much pride to confess their weaknesses. I'll tell you it's a good thing to get some of your weaknesses out of your system by confession. Acknowledge that maybe you're not perfect - well, not entirely perfect. Maybe the other fellow will say, come to think of it neither am I, and then you're off to the races.

Rededicate yourself to a better relationship with the people that you come into contact everyday, whoever they may be. What a wonderful thing it is. You can do that, you can handle it; you can handle it, I know you can! You know, most of these inharmonies in human relations is due to the neglect of people. You just neglect to build up your human relations. You could do it if you wanted to do it.

And, the budgeting of income and expenses so as to provide for the accumulation of a definite amount for old age and security of loved ones and so forth, and the budgeting of time so as to provide whatever income that is necessary to support one's plan for the attainment of a definite major purpose; that should be a part of a definite major purpose.

Write out your platform of life, and include down under these minor purposes: The things that are related to your major purpose, the things that you're going to have to get in the step-by-step movement up toward your major purpose.

And a definite plan for developing harmony in all your relations, and especially these: In the home, where one works, where one plays or relaxes. The human relationship plank is the most important one in connection with one's major aim since the aim is attainable very largely through the cooperation of others.

Had you ever thought of that, that the things that you do in life, if they're worthwhile, have to be done through harmonious cooperation with other people?

And how are you going to get that harmonious cooperation if you don't cultivate people, if you don't understand them, if you don't make allowances for their weaknesses? Did you ever have a friend that appreciated your trying to reform him or change his mind about something? Do you like to have a friend come around and try to reform you? No, you don't. Nobody does.

But there are certain things you can do for a friend by example -- that's a mighty effective way of doing it. But start in and tell a man where he's wrong, the chances are that he'll beat us around the corner. The next time he sees you coming he'll get on the other side of the street.

In your human relations, you can develop a marvelous relationship but you can't do it by criticizing people, harping upon their faults, because we all have faults. A better thing to do is to talk about a person's virtues and his good qualities. I have never seen a person yet so lowly that he didn't have some good qualities, and if you'll concentrate upon those good qualities, that person on whom you're concentrating will go out of his way and lean over backwards to make sure that you're not disappointed.

One should not hesitate to choose a major aim which may be, for the time being, out of his reach, for one may always prepare himself to attain pretty much any desired purpose in life. Certainly, when I chose as my definite major purpose the organizing and taking to the world of the first practical philosophy of individual achievement, it was way beyond my reach. And what do you think it was that kept me down to twenty years of unproductive effort of research? What do you think it was that kept me striving and struggling in face of the fact the majority of people I knew were criticizing me? What do you think it was?

I had to have an abundance of faith, and I had to keep that faith alive by moving, moving always, as if I knew in advance that I was going to complete the task which Mr. Carnegie assigned to me. There were times when it looked as if what my friends and relatives were saying about me was absolutely true. And in a sense it was, that I was wasting my time. From their viewpoint and their measuring stick and standards, I was wasting twenty years of my time. But from the viewpoint of the millions of people who have benefited and will benefit by my work during those twenty years, I was not wasting my time.

You can't fail! Unless you think you can. If you think you can fail, then you can. But if you stay around me long enough I'll get you so you're not going to think you're going to fail. You'll know you're not going to fail.

Our greatest demonstration of the universal application of the principle of definiteness of purpose may be seen by observing how nature applies it as follows -- and there is a great string of applications the way nature moves with definiteness of purpose. And ladies and gentlemen, if there is anything in this universe that's definite, it's the laws of nature. They don't deviate, they don't temporize, they don't subside, you can't go around them, you can't avoid them, and however you can learn their nature and adjust yourselves to them and benefit by them, nobody ever heard of the law of gravitation being suspended, not even for one fraction of a second. It never has been done and never will be, because nature's whole setup, throughout the whole universe -- system of universes perhaps -- is so definite that everything moves with precision, like clockwork.

If you want an example of the necessity of an individual's

moving with definiteness, you only have to have a smattering of understanding of the sciences to see the way that nature does things, and then you'll have that example. The orderliness of the universe and the interrelation of all of the natural laws, the fixation of all of the stars and planets in immovable relationship to one another; isn't it a marvelous thing to know that the astronomers can sit down and with a pencil and a few pieces of paper and predetermine hundreds of years in advance the exact relationship of given planets and stars, right where they'll be with relationship to one another? In advance!

And you know they couldn't do that if there was not a purpose, a plan under which we're working. We want to find out what that purpose is as it relates to us as individuals. That's why you're in this course, that's why I'm teaching you; I'm giving you that little bit that I've picked up from life and from the experiences of men and from my own experience, so that you will learn how to adjust yourself to the laws of nature in order that you may use those laws instead of allowing yourself to be abused by your neglect in using them.

To me, one of the most horrible things to contemplate is the possible cessation of natural laws. Imagine all of the chaos, all of the stars and planets running together while they make the H-bomb look like a firecracker, if nature allowed her laws to be suspended. But she doesn't do that. She has very definite laws to go by, and you'll find that if you check these seventeen principles, they check perfectly with all of the laws of nature.

You know that principle of going the extra mile? You'll find that nature is profound in her application of the principle of going the extra mile. When she produces blooms on the trees, she doesn't produce just enough to fill the tree, she produces enough to take care of all of the damages from the winds and the storms. When she produces fish in the sea, she doesn't just produce enough to perpetuate the fish, she produces enough to feed the bullfrogs and the snakes and the alligators, and all the other things and still have enough left to carry out her purpose. She has an abundance of things -- overabundance. And also, she forces man to go the extra mile or else he'll perish. He would perish in one season if he didn't go the extra mile. If nature didn't compensate a man when he goes and puts a grain of wheat in the ground by giving him back 500 grains to compensate him for his intelligence, why we'd starve to death in one season.

If you do your part, nature does her part, and she does it in abundance; in superabundance.

And one of the strange things about nature is that if you keep your mind focused on the positive side of life, it becomes greater than the negative side. It always does that.

If you keep your mind on the positive side, it becomes greater than all of the negatives that may try to penetrate your mind and influence your life.

Look around and you'll find examples, living examples, all around you of people that you want to emulate and people you do not want to emulate -- people that are failing, and you'll be able to tell why they're failing.

I dare say that from this time on, you will be able to use this philosophy as a measuring stick at wherever you find a success or a failure. You'll be able to lay your

finger right on the cause of it --
right on, and that includes you
too.

We have Book Recommendations for you

The Power of Your Subconscious
Mind by Joseph Murphy
MP3 [UNABRIDGED]
(Audio CD)

Think and Grow Rich [MP3
AUDIO] [UNABRIDGED]
by Napoleon Hill, Jason McCoy
(Narrator) (Audio CD)

As a Man Thinketh
[UNABRIDGED]
by James Allen, Jason McCoy
(Narrator) (Audio CD)

Automatic Wealth I, The Secrets of the Millionaire Mind- Including: As a Man Thinketh, The Science of Getting Rich, The Way to Wealth and Think and Grow Rich (Paperback)

The Bestsellers on this Book give sound advice about money or how to obtain it. Just shoot to the stars and stay focused on your dreams and it will happen. There is nothing that we can imagine, that we can't do. So what are we waiting for, let's begin the journey of self- fullfillment.

4 Bestsellers in 1 Book:

As a Man Thinketh by James Allen

The Science of Getting Rich by Wallace D. Wattles,

The Way to Wealth by Benjamin Franklin

Think and Grow Rich by Napoleon Hill

BN Publishing

Improving People's Life

www.bnpublishing.com

BN Publishing

Improving People's Life

www.bnpublishing.com

Printed in the United States
85823LV00001B/166-168/A